D1400261

DATE DUE

DEMCO 38-297

How to Draw

Sports

Things

For Jesse, Jasmine, Justin, Jordan, Melina, and Matthew

Published in the United States of America by The Child's World®
1980 Lookout Drive • Mankato, MN 56003-1705
800-599-READ • www.childsworld.com

Acknowledgments
Illustration and Design: Rob Court
Production: The Creative Spark, San Juan Capistrano, CA

Registration

Library of Congress Cataloging-in-Publication Data
Court, Rob, 1956–
  How to draw sports things / by Rob Court.
    p. cm. — (Doodle books)
  ISBN 978-1-59296-956-2 (library bound : alk. paper)
 1. Sports in art—Juvenile literature. 2. Sports—Equipment and supplies—
Juvenile literature. 3. Drawing—Technique—Juvenile literature. I. Title. II.
Series.

NC825.S62C69 2008
743'.89796—dc22

2007013394

The Scribbles Institute ™

How to Draw

Sports

Things

by Rob Court

The Child's World®

basketball

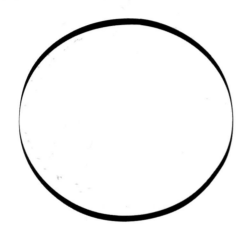

1

2

3

4

bat

1

2

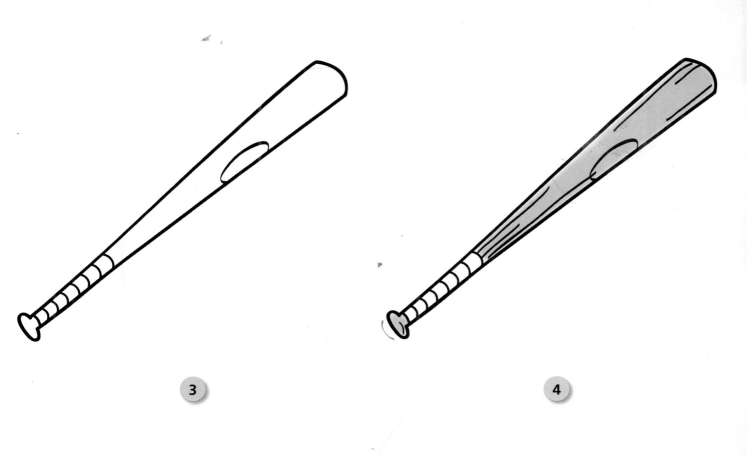

3

4

bicycle helmet

1

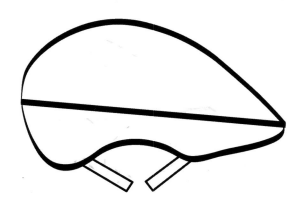

2

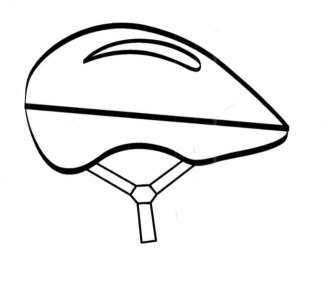

3

4

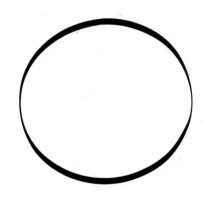

1

2

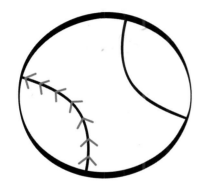

3

4

surfboard

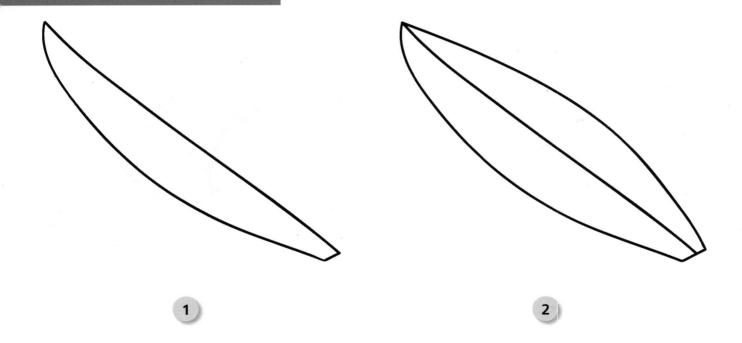

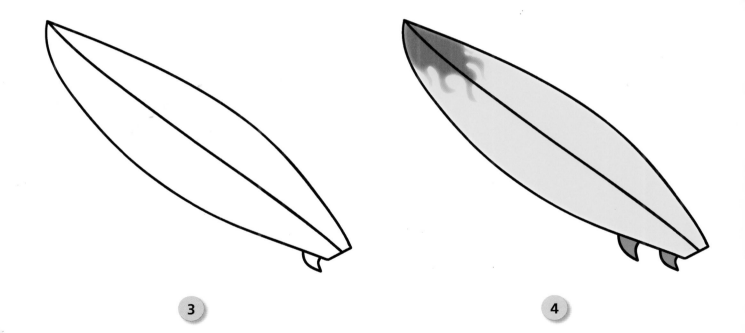

3

4

soccer ball

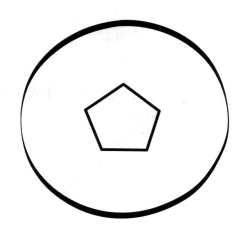

1

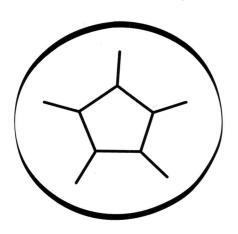

2

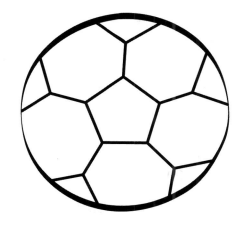

3

4

golf club

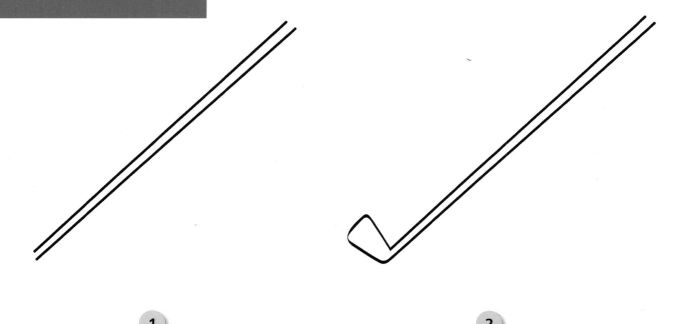

1

2

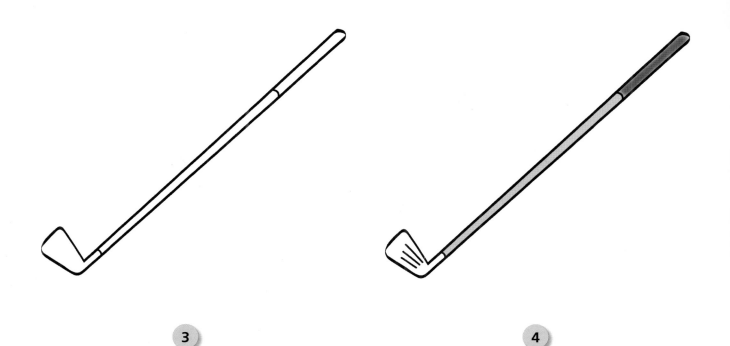

3

4

football

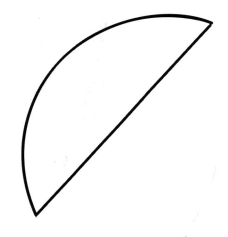

1

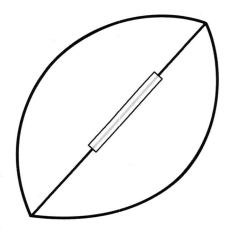

2

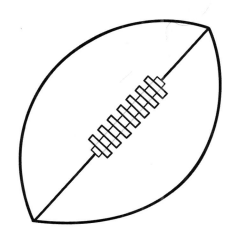

3

4

tennis racket

1

2

3

4

baseball glove

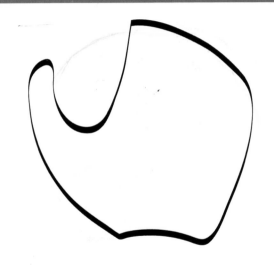

1

2

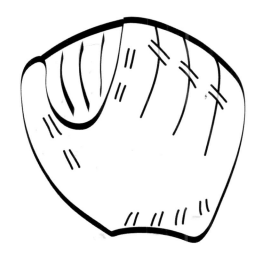

3

4

football helmet

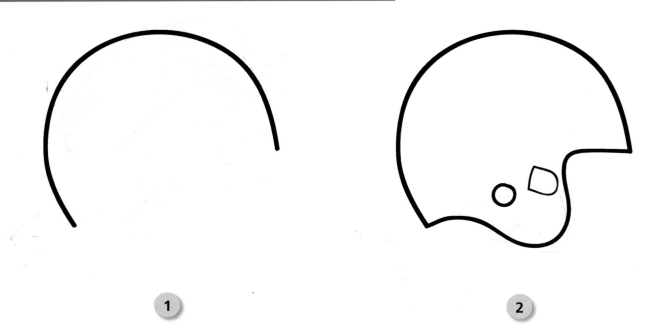

1

2

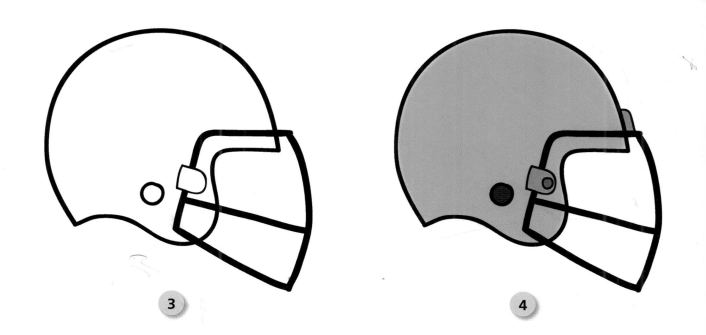

skateboard

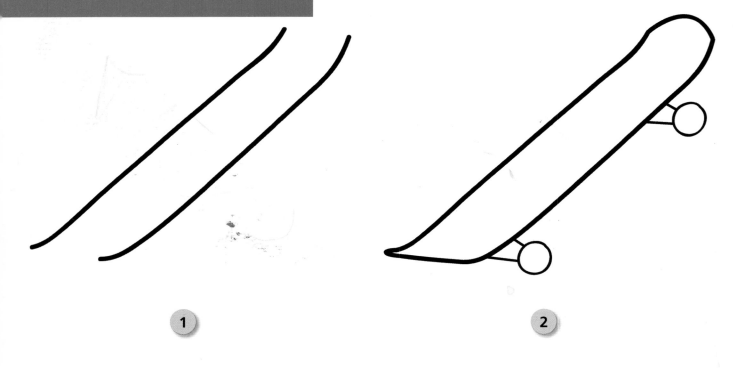

1

2

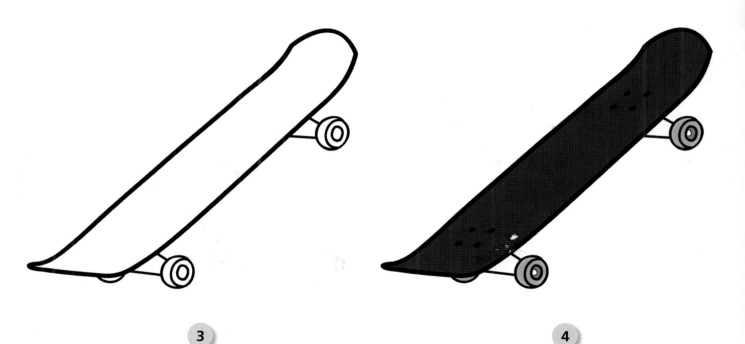

3

4

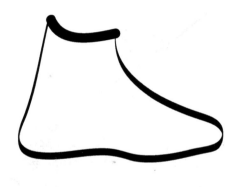

1

2

3

4

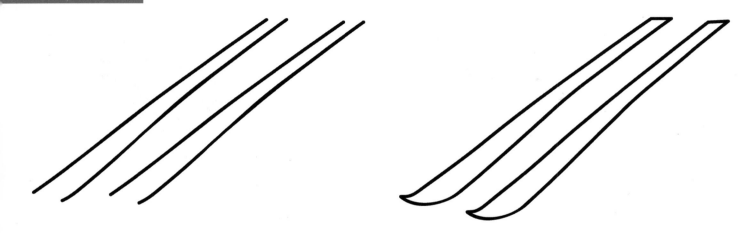

1

2

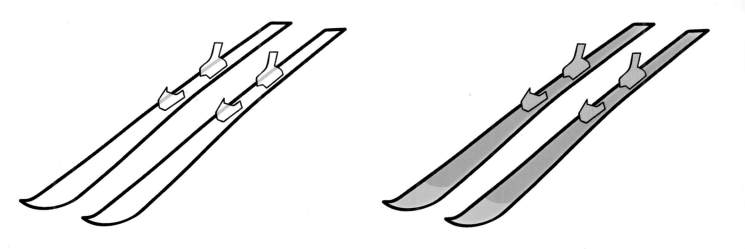

3

4

lines

 horizontal

 vertical

angled

curved

thick

thin

 dotted

 • point

squiggly

dashed

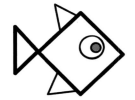

Move a point to make a line.

Connect lines to make a shape.

Shapes make all kinds of wonderful things!

loop

Repeating dots, lines, and shapes makes patterns.

About the Author

Rob Court is a graphic artist and illustrator. He started the Scribbles Institute to help students, parents, and teachers learn about drawing and visual art. Please visit www.scribblesinstitute.com

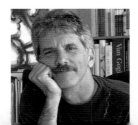